The River Of Life
El Río De La Vida
Journal ~ Diario

Written and Illustrated by Gabriella Eva Nagy

Copyright© 2016 Gabriella Eva Nagy
Illustrated by Gabriella Eva Nagy
All rights reserved.

No part of this book may be reproduced in any manner without the written consent of the publisher except for brief excerpts in critical reviews or articles.

ISBN 13: 978-1-61244-508-3

Printed in the United States of America

Published by Halo Publishing International
1100 NW Loop 410
Suite 700 - 176
San Antonio, Texas 78213
Toll Free 1-877-705-9647
www.halopublishing.com
www.holapublishing.com
e-mail: contact@halopublishing.com

*Revelation 22 is the inspiration of this devotional.
The holiness of God is manifested
through His love, power, and purity.*

THE RIVER OF LIFE

And he showed me a pure river of water of life, clear as crystal,
proceeding from the throne of God and of the Lamb.

In the middle of its street, and on either side of the river, was the tree of life, which bore twelve fruits, each tree yielding its fruit every month. The leaves of the tree were for the healing of the nations.

And there shall be no more curse, but the throne of God and of the Lamb shall be in it, and His servants shall serve Him.

They shall see His face, and His name shall be on their foreheads.
There shall be no night there: They need no lamp nor light of the sun, for the Lord God gives them light. And they shall reign forever and ever.

Revelation 22: 1-5. (NKJV)

EL RÍO DE LA VIDA

Después me mostró un río de agua de
vida, resplandeciente como cristal,
que fluye del trono de Dios y
y del Cordero.

En medio de la avenida de la ciudad, y a
uno y otro lado del Río, está el árbol de la
vida, que produce doce frutos, dando
cada mes su fruto. Las
hojas del árbol son para la sanidad
de las naciones.

Ya no habrá más maldición, y
el trono de Dios y del Cordero
estará en ella, y sus siervos le
rendirán culto.

Verán su rostro, y Su nombre
estará en sus frentes.
No Habrá Más noche, ni tienen necesidad
de luz de Lámpara, ni de luz del sol; porque
el Señor Dios alumbrará sobre ellos, y
y reinarán por los siglos de los siglos.

Revelación 22:1-5